THE SECRET

To The Best Life

(How to find it & how to Live It)

MOHAMED IDRIS

TABLE OF CONTENTS

ABOUT THIS BOOK

This book was first drafted in 2000 while I was living in the City of Atlanta, Georgia. Quite a long time ago, isn't it? The draft remained in my files, for editing and finalizing, until I moved from Atlanta to Columbus, OH in 2003. This was the time I was participating in the establishment of Ibnu Taymiyah Masjid and Islamic Center.

Since then, I couldn't find any copy of the draft, hard or digital, and of course, this was long before the social media revolution along with its clouds and file saving. Therefore, I had to come to terms with the fact that the draft was a lost effort.

Recently, while I was looking through some documents in my library, my daughter Muna raised a small plastic folder, and said: "What about this?" As soon as I saw the title, I was astonished to see the draft that I had lost 15 years earlier. I understood that now was the time for it, perhaps a better timing than 15 years earlier.

I have printed many books in different languages, but this one, although small in size, is great in content, or at least I think so. The fact that I poured my heart into it, makes it one of the closest books to me.

Now I want to share with the readers around the world my journey in finding what the best life could be and what the joy of life can look like in our reality.

I have no doubt that the definition of "best life" can differ from one person to another, and it's experienced differently from various aspects and angles.

However, I'm also aware that all of us, millions of people from different backgrounds, different levels of knowledge, scientists, professors, executives, politicians, writers, business tycoons, and the ordinary workers are all searching or looking for a glimpse of what the best life could be.

This concept has been chased for centuries, in different places, through different beliefs, religions, and cultures, and still, the question remains haunting many people around the world and the search isn't near finished.

It is an ancient question that's still relevant in the modern world: How I can feel the joy and happiness of life? I think it is a legitimate question, and everybody has the right to live it and find it. Unfortunately, many of us could not achieve that dream, or could not find it, even if it is very close to them, and wouldn't cost them anything besides a little effort.

Therefore, let us take a step back and try to look deeper into this old question for one more time. Who knows? It might be exactly what somebody, somewhere needs, or at least that's what I hope.

Seeking success and happiness can be a long and tiring journey, but the sparkling change comes in only a minute. This is the minute you decide to taste the best life. It is the minute you decide to live with the only and real source of the best life.

It is very simple. Logically speaking, whoever can give us life, knows how to give us the best of it. The one who creates life can therefore create the joy and happiness within it. No One else can give the best as he can. The maker of the product can come up with its best manual. Pretty fair and logical, don't you think?

M. Idris

ENJOYING THE BEST LIFE

FOREWORD

Each one of us goes through life seeking to make it the best we can but everyone has a different definition of what the best life actually means. So which definition is true? What is the real best life? How we can introduce it, explain it, and therefore explain how to find it? What does it feel like to be living the best life? What are the criteria that make a good life differ from a bad one?

Is the good life measured by what we have in our bank account? Is it defined by good health, even if you are poor? Is it to have a good job, high income, beloved wife/husband, and beautiful house? Is it in finding the fun in everything, going to dinners, being the life of each part, being a superstar in the media, being rich and famous?

Our imaginations might soar wild when it comes to answering this vital question. However, we may still not agree on how to interpret the best life. You may see it from one side, and I see the other. You may feel it in one way and I may feel it another, and this can go on forever.

Actually, this contradiction is not true. It may seem that the best life has many meanings or definitions and that it differs from one to another. However, if we took a closer look, we will find there's no contradiction at all.

The best life is the best and it has one meaning and this is because mankind is of one origin despite our different languages, religions, environments, and cultures. In the end, we all have the same need for food, drink, sex, and fun, etc. Deep down, we all have the same biological build-up, structure, and content, no matter where we come from. Mankind is one, and we all come down to the same natural habits and human psychology.

I would like, however, to emphasize and offer the way I see the best life. The way I think it is. I hope it will be interesting for everyone chasing the best life.

All people are looking for the best life. The one working on the farm, and the other who is in the sea. The one squeezing his brain on how to make more money, and the one who already achieved a high level of wealth and job integrity.

A person going to school and another chasing crack in the street are both desperate to find the best life in their different ways, but where is this valuable thing that we are all seeking?

A serious searcher of the truth, who later found the best life by embracing Islam, said in his story:

(I once thought my upbringing offered an excellent way of life, especially since I felt satisfied both mentally and physically. As a young man, I lived the life of an average American who had a rather hedonistic lifestyle; I was fond of music, a festive atmosphere games, sports, travel, ethnic foods, and foreign languages.

I reached, however, a point, where I felt "spiritually bankrupt" and I asked myself, "now what?" And I thought, "there has to be more life than this". This realization was the impetus that led me to search for the truth through diverse avenues".[1]

I hope, therefore, that I can help shed some light on the way to find the best life and enjoy both your life and death.

Mohamed Idris

---

[1]) Best way to live and die - Yahya - Donald Flood

Chapter 1

BELIEVE IN (ALLAH) AND FORGET THE REST!

I encourage you to do one thing: stand up for a moment and think. Who created you? Why did he create you? What is the purpose of your creation? And where are we going after this life?

We see every day and month and year thousands and millions of people leaving this life and never coming back to life, friends, relatives, loved ones. Is that the end?

What is the real future and what's the end of this journey in life? Who is watching over and governing everything in this universe, both the seen and the unseen parts of it? Were you given a choice to come to this life, when to come, and when and how to leave it? Have you had the option to choose your father or mother? your color or country and language? your face and race?

On the other end, do you have a choice regarding the date when you'll (leave) this world behind? The way, the place, and the time you will leave it? Do you have the knowledge or information about what would happen after this life? And what is the authentic source to rely on this information?

There are some questions here one may ask to understand his situation and location on this map.

If you can answer these questions carefully and perfectly, I hope that you will come close to reality and thus to the source of the Best Life.

However, I am glad to say that the true and one answer to these questions is in one word only: ALLAH. The only God who deserves to be worshipped.

Simply put, he is the one who created us, the one who provides us, the one who feeds us from heaven and earth, the one who governs this world, both the seen and the unseen parts of it.

He is the only one, to whom we return after death, and will meet to ask us what we have done with our time in this world.

To believe in ALLAH the only God, Lord, who deserves to be worshipped alone, the creator, the sustainer, the raiser, and the giver means to come closer to discovering what the Best Life is.

You have a very simple formula: If Allah is the one who created this soul, then the best life can only be felt with its Creator.

**Read and Listen to this Verse from the last revelation,
The Qur'an:**

((Does not man see that We have created him from Nutfah (mixed male and female discharge - semen drops). Yet behold! He (stands forth) as an open opponent. And he puts forth for us a parable and forgets his own creation. He says: "Who will give life to these bones when they have rotted away and became dust?". Say: He will give life to them Who created for the first time! And He is All knower of every creation!"). [2]

Think about small things in your own life that will make your soul full of happiness and pleasure. Who saved you nine months in the womb of your mother? Who equipped you with, the tongue to speak and taste before you came to the world? The eyes to see and distinguish? The brain to think, memorize, analyze and judge in seconds? Who brought you to this world and to whom will you surrender back in the end?

Allah Almighty is the only one who rendered you with all the above and many more. But what is the purpose? What is the objective and the goal?

The answer is in the Qur'an: *(And I created not the Jinns and humans except they should worship Me (alone).* [3]

---

[2]) Sura 36 (77-83)
[3]) Sura 51-56

You are not created and fitted with all the blessings without purpose and mission, and it is quite an important mission, to worship sincerely Allah alone and submit to him.

Another question that rings our ears: *(Did you think that we had created you in play (without any purpose) and that you would not be brought back to us).*[4]

This is a question that weighs heavily on your shoulder. It's up to you to find the true answer, seriously, fairly, truly, and precisely. It is not a small matter so there's no room for doubts or guesses. It is where your real future lies.

Therefore, you have to make sure that you have an authentic source of knowledge and information. Nevertheless, I can assure you that the answer can't be found anywhere outside the only source that can give you the full knowledge, that is the one who made you. That is Allah, and what he revealed to his Messengers like, Abraham, Moses, Jesus, and Muhammad, peace, and blessings may be upon them all. They, themselves, did not have any knowledge except what Allah had taught them, and you can find these answers in the Qur'an, the last revelation of Allah to mankind.

There are some who knew this true faith, genuine path, authentic source, but they deny it due to jealousy and arrogance. On the other

---

[4]) Sura 23-115

hand, there are some who don't know the truth, follow their teachers blindly, and are ultimately misled.

All the numerous instruments granted to you by Allah are to be thought, judged, and be thankful to him. Listen to this and take a moment to ponder on what it means:

(And Allah has brought you out from the wombs of your mothers, while you know nothing, and he gave you hearing, sight, and hearts that you might give thanks (to Allah).[5]

It's a serious situation with no room for joke. On my end, I am not attempting to interpret, but just trying to convey to you the word of Allah, the revelation to his Messenger (peace be upon him). The words of Allah are not like others. It is powerful, supreme, filled with facts, spirit, and truth, especially when you read and understand it fully in its original language, which is Arabic, in the case of the last revelation, The Qur'an.

It penetrates the hearts, goes directly to the soul so that we can not only understand it but also feel it. And live it. Listen to this strong message:

((Allah knows what every female bears, and by how much the wombs fall short (of their time or number) or exceed. Everything with him is in (due) proportion. All-knower of the unseen and seen, the Most Great, Most High. It is the same (to him) whether any of

---

[5]) Sura 16-78

you conceal his speech or declare it openly, whether he be hid by night or go forth freely by day. For each person (person), there are angels in succession, before and behind him. They guard him by the command of Allah. Verily, Allah will not change the good condition of a people as long as they do not change their state of goodness (by committing sins and being ungrateful and disobedient to Allah). But when Allah will people's punishment, there can be no turning back of it, and they will find besides him no protector.)[6]

This is the fact. You are under constant surveillance for 24 hours. The angels are witnessing and recording everything you do. The whole nature, the day, the night, the earth, and the heaven will be witnessing your actions. If you make any objection or try to reject those witnesses, your own body, your hands, your legs, your skin, and your tongue will be a witness that cannot be rejected.

Listen to this verse where Allah is reminding us to be cautious:

(On the day when their tongues, their hands, and their legs or feet will bear witness against them as to what they used to do. On that day Allah will pay them the recompense of their deeds in full, and they will know that Allah, - He is the Manifest Truth).[7]

And in another Chapter, Allah has repeated the reminding to assure you this fact and make it firm and present in your heart at all times:

---

[6]) Sura 13 -(8-11)
[7]) Sura 24 (24-25)

((And (remember) the Day that the enemies of Allah will be gathered to the Fire, so they will be collected there (the first and the last). Till, when they reach it (Hell-fire), their hearing (ears) and their eyes, and their skins will testify against them as to what they used to do. And they will say to their skins: "why do you testify against us?" They will say: "Allah has caused us to speak, as he causes all things to speak, and he created you the first time, and to Him you are made to return." And you have not been hiding against yourselves, lest your ears, and your eyes, and your skins testify against you, but you thought That Allah knew not much of you were doing. And that thought of yours which you thought about your Lord, has brought you to destruction, and you have become (this day) of those utterly lost!)).[8]

These implications can show you the wisdom behind the idea. I can feel calm knowing that I believe in God. I can enjoy life with a persistent soul, as long as I observe his commands, obey his rules, follow his revelation, and practice the deeds and duties assigned to me.

Ultimately, the result is that I *feel* the best life that a human could possibly taste or exercise. The Master of the body is the heart, and the heart is in your chest but it's also in the hands of the Creator. It is the center where all happiness and sorrows come from. It can be happy and pleased only with the remembrance of the Creator, Allah.

---

[8]) Sura 41(19-23)

The heart cannot be shared by two, Allah and the Devil. Because the Devil is the enemy of the man, he wants him to be as far as possible from Allah and wishes to conquer his heart. On the other hand, Allah wants you to be with him, both in your mind and heart, so that he can defend you against the Devil and his evil.

((Those who believe (in the Oneness of Allah - Islamic Monotheism), and whose hearts find rest in the remembrance of Allah. Verily, in the remembrance of Allah do hearts find rest)).[9]

This belief in Allah, truly, genuinely, and perfectly, knowing him and remembering him is the only way that can lead you to the best life.

First, you must know your position and that you are in this world to worship Allah, and believe in His angels, Books, Messengers, and the day of resurrection (hereafter) when mankind will be judged, and that whatever happens to you good & evil is according to the creed of Allah.

Second, you will prepare for that situation.

Third, you will have good knowledge of your Creator and will obey him according to the teaching of the Qur'an and the teachings of the last Messenger Muhammad (peace be upon him), and therefore your heart will rest and be on its way to enjoy the best life.

---

[9]) Sura 13-28

Chapter 2

TAKE A LOOK AT THE AMAZING UNIVERSE AROUND YOU & FEEL THE SIGNS!

O n my way to the best life, I had to go back and take a look at nature and the universe around me, the countless parts of this world which accompany me, each day and each moment.

How I can neglect these heavens covering over me as a roof without pillars or columns, no holes, no curves or cracks, or twists?

How can I ignore this sun, which rises every day from the same location and time? It's never absent and never a minute late, there is no mistake in it doing its job, and it supplies us with power, energy, light, and health.

This moon, which lightens the whole world like a huge lamp, on a certain fixed time every month, winds coming back and forth, if it speeds more than its natural speed it will destroy everything by the orders of its creator.

How can we go through life ignoring the sea and oceans? It gives us endless fresh food, ornaments, and through it we transport our goods globally on huge ships, seeking business and wealth. (Keep in mind that at the time of globalization era, the largest global transportation is thru the sea, and the largest 10 ports in the world transfer yearly 250 million containers to more than 800 ports around the world). [10]

These huge mountains, valleys, and flat land, the gardens and deserts, trees and grass, the birds and animals, war and peace, rich and poor, happiness and grief, cries and laughter, deaths and births, who is behind all these? Who is governing and administering this wide nature?

These few minutes of rational thinking about this world and nature will make you recognize, thank, acknowledge and be grateful to Allah, who is the only one behind all these scenes.

He continually invites us to look around, and think about the universe. This is one of the best ways Allah introduces himself to his servants. It is the best way to strengthen your belief and to taste the best life.

((Who has created the seven heavens one above another, you can see no fault in the creation of the Most Gracious. Then look again:

---

[10]) World Economic Forum website

"Can you see any rifts?". *Then look again and yet again, your sight will return to you in a state of humiliation and worn out)).* [11]

That is only to remind us to look around, to refresh our minds and hearts, so we may indeed increase our understanding of the secrets for true belief and happiness:

((Have they not looked at the heaven above them, how We have made it and adorned it, and there are no rifts in it? And the earth! We have spread it out, and set thereon mountains standing firm, and have produced therein every kind of lovely growth "plants")). [12]

((Do they not look at the Camels how they are created? And the Heavens how it is raised? And the mountains how they are rooted and fixed firm? And at the earth how it is spread out? So remind them you are only One who reminds)). [13]

Who is to be reminded? It is you and I , he and she, and all of us, mankind as a whole. The reminder is not particular to Muslims, it's relatable to everyone who wants to listen and heed.

Generally, the Qur'an itself is not addressed to only Muslims; it is addressed to mankind as a whole. It is the last revelation from Allah, the Almighty, and the last word conveyed to us by his last messenger. It tells the history of those who came before us: The

---

[11]) Surah 67 (2-3)
[12]) Surah 50 (6-7)
[13]) Surah 88 (17-21)

prophets, the nations, the Jews and Christians and how they're specially treated, the story of Moses, Jesus, Abraham, Noah, and many other Prophets that Allah sent to the people.

All of them from Noah to Muhammad (peace be upon them) were calling for the same faith and carrying the same message. They are our brothers, who took guidance from the same source, Allah. The Qur'an tells us, therefore, the true history of this world, the judgment between us, the news of the future hereafter, all in full knowledgeable and most reliable information.

It summarizes the complete journey of the man, from the beginning to the end.

((We created man from the finest extract of clay; then we placed him as a sperm in a firmly established lodging; then we fashioned the sperm into an embryo, then fashioned the embryo into a shapeless lump of flesh; then from the lump of flesh We fashioned bones, then clothed the bones with flesh. Thus we informed him into new creation. So blessed be God the best of Creators. And then you will certainly die; Then will be raised up on the Day of Resurrection)). [14]

The Qur'an discusses the matter to all people in general, since it is a message to all mankind. In a way, it says: "O Mankind; O sons of Adam, it is from the Lord who knows you in your particular name, identity, since you were in the womb of your mother."

---

[14]) Surah 23 (12-14)

You will verily meet him on the day of judgment, and he will definitely ask you about everything you have done in this world, between you and him.

You will be asked about the Qur'an, Islam, the Prophet, the guidance and rules of the Qur'an. It is therefore your own decision and you will be held full responsibility. There is absolutely no compulsion for Islam, no practicing it by force or pressure. Allah mentioned explicitly in the Qur'an:

((There is no compulsion in the religion. Verily the Right Path has became distinct than the wrong path)). [15]

The dazzling nature around us is a clear sign of the Creator. The whole universe worships Allah and is obedient to Him, except the many people who don't submit to Him.

((Do you not see that to Allah prostrates whoever is in the heavens and whoever is on the earth and the sun, the moon, the stars, the mountains, the trees, the moving creatures and many of the people? But upon many the punishment has been justified. An he whom Allah humiliates - for him there is no bestower of honor. Indeed, Allah does what he wills). [16]

We can note from the verse that upon mentioning all creatures, there was no exception in their worship and prostration to Allah,

---

[15]) Surah 2-256
[16]) Surah 22 - 18

but when the people (mankind) were mentioned, there was an exception that some of them prostrate and some of them not.

The main reason is that Allah Almighty has given mankind free will, and with it comes the liberty to believe in Him or not, while other creatures don't have this option.

It's an undeniable fact that every creature worships Allah. However, we cannot understand how they worship, how they glorify Allah, or how they express themselves.

No human can understand except those who Allah gave them the language of these creatures. For instance, Prophet-King David, (Da'ud) in the Qur'an, Solomon, (Suleiman) in the Qur'an, were among those Allah taught to understand the language of these mountains, trees, animals, and insects and therefore, understand how they worship Allah.

((Verily, We made the mountains to glorify Our Praises with him, David, Da'ud, after the mid-day till sunset, and so did the birds assembled all with him did turn to Allah). [17]

((And Sulaiman (Solomon) inherited "the knowledge" of Da'ud (David). He said O mankind, we have been taught the language of bird, and on us have been bestowed all things. This, verily, is an evident grace "from Allah")). [18]

---

[17]) Surah 38 (18-19)

[18]) Surah 27 (16)

Accordingly, Sulaiman, peace be upon him, was able to speak with the Jinns, Birds, Ants etc., and understand their conversation.

They were all his hosts, they served him in every aspect, in the sea, in the land, and the air. The winds were traveling on his demand, taking him to wherever he required in a short time. That was a gift from Allah Almighty.

((And indeed we bestowed grace on David from Us "saying" O you mountains, Glorify "Allah" with him. And you Birds "also", and we made the iron soft for him)).[19]

((And to Solomon "we subjected" the wind, its morning "stride from sunrise till mid-noon", and its afternoon "stride from the mid-day decline of the sun to sunset) was a month's journey "i.e. in one day he could travel two month's journey". And we caused a fount of "molten" brass to flow for him, and there were jinns that worked in front of him, by the Leave of his Lord, and whosoever of them turned aside from Our Command, We shall cause him to taste of the torment of the blazing Fire. They worked for him what he desired, "making" high rooms, images, basins as large as reservoirs, and cooking cauldrons fixed "in their places". Work you, O family of Da'ud "David", with thanks! But few of My slaves are grateful)).[20]

---

[19]) Surah 34-10
[20]) Surah 34 (12-13)

This entire world is for Allah, and no one participates in this ownership and his order.

Looking around you and thinking thoroughly about matters of this universe is very important and we, in fact, have been asked to do so. This is one of the ways we can reach the required results by ourselves and reach the conclusion that Allah is the Creator and that only he has the right to be worshipped. It is how we can believe in his names and attributes, which indicates that *((There is nothing like unto Him, He is the All-Hearer, All-Seer)).*[21]

The signs and proofs that Allah is the Creator and the only one to be worshipped are surrounding you all over in the world. Allah with his mercy asked us to watch the world, to watch ourselves, to see the universe and the pieces of evidence everywhere.

((We will show them Our signs in the universe, and in their own selves until it becomes manifest to them that this (the Qur'an) is the truth. Is it not sufficient in regard to your Lord that He is a Witness over all things?)).[22]

((Do they not look in the domination of the heavens and the earth and all things that Allah has created, and that it may be that the

---

[21]) Surah 42-11
[22]) Surah 42-53.

end of their lives is near. In what message after this will they then believe?)).[23]

What message after this last revelation could we be waiting for to believe in Allah and worship Him alone? We can't go back in time and make up for the time lost, so you have to believe in Allah, and act according to this belief by following what Allah has ordained in his book of Qur'an and forbidding what Allah has prohibited to save ourselves from Hell's agony.

Then the formula is very simple: In order to find and taste the best life we have to believe in Allah, the Almighty. To genuinely believe in Allah, we have to look at the signs and the proof of his greatness in the amazing universe around us. Finally, to be able to understand and communicate with this miraculous universe around us everywhere, we must truly open our hearts, keep our minds open and think out of the box.

---

[23]) Surah 7-185.

Chapter 3

ONLY TRUE BELIEVERS TASTE THE BEST LIFE!

The first believers of Allah in mankind were the Prophets (Messengers) in the first row and their Companions and followers in the second line. The Companions of Prophet Muhammad (peace be upon him) are the most extinguished generation who implemented the true faith in the best – and the most practical - way of life.

They got the chance to experience the best life because they had the best knowledge of Allah straight from the Prophets. Therefore, we can understand how whenever the knowledge of Allah increases, the level of the faith becomes higher, and the taste of this best life becomes sweeter.

They tasted the best life because they believed in Allah, and they recognized Him and worshipped Him, day and night, and in all aspects of their life.

They tasted the best life because they understood the meaning of life and death, and they worked hard to prepare with their good deeds.

They tasted the best life because they watched what Allah had created in the world around them, and they feared Him strictly adhered to His Commands.

They tasted the best life because they spent their time worshipping Allah and remembering him at all times and in all aspects of their life. Whether they were at work, in their home, the street, or anywhere else, they watched Allah and were thankful to him.

They tasted the best life because they experienced real liberty. Today, man believes that he has freedom when he can do whatever he likes. However, that is not what true freedom means in reality.

True freedom is becoming a slave to Allah Only, the creator, and it's found in fully submitting to him. That is when you are free of becoming a slave to any other thing in this world.

The people who run away from Allah and reject or ignore his commands and the restrictions of the religion, fall into the worst slavery a man can see. They slowly become slaves for themselves, their environment, the material things they own, lust, and so on.

True freedom and liberty are different than what you may imagine or interpret. Sometimes you may become - voluntarily - a slave for your desire or for some norms of your society if you believe that you cannot do or live without it.

The Qur'an says:

((Have you seen the one who takes as his God his own desire? Then would you have been responsible for him?)).[24]

The qualifications to the best life can be summarized in the following two conditions:

1. Faith (To believe in Allah) – all the time, anywhere, in every generation.
2. Doing good deeds

Anyone who fulfills these two conditions, male or female, will definitely enjoy his life, both in this world and thereafter. Allah Said in the Qur'an:

((Whoever works righteousness, whether male or female, while he (or she) s a true believer (of Islamic Monotheism) verily to him We will give a good life (in this world with respect, contentment, and lawful provision), and We shall pay them certainly a reward in proportion to the best of what they used to do (i.e. Paradise in the Hereafter).)).[25]

---

[24]) Sura 25 (43)
[25]) Sura 16-97

Chapter 4

THINK THOROUGHLY? WHAT ARE YOU REALLY ABOUT?!

It is a matter of fact that you have to think thoroughly, just to be sure whether you are on the right path or not.

You have to seek and search for the truth, to save yourself from the Hellfire, and to have the chance to make your destination in paradise, which people are competing for.

The idea of salvation without price is not working. Moreover, it has never existed in the revealed religions in their true and original verses.

The Old Testament, The Gospel, and finally the Qur'an have called the man to be obedient to Allah, the Creator. According to Jesus (peace be upon him), man is saved through obedience and submission to Allah, and he never asked to be worshipped.

The Holy Qur'an calls the Christians:

((O people of the scripture! Do not exceed the limits in your religion, nor say of Allah aught but the truth. The Messiah "Issa" (Jesus) son of Maryam (Mary) was no more than a Messenger of Allah and His word, (Be and he was) which He bestowed on Maryam and a spirit created by Him, so believe in Allah and His Messengers. Say not: Three (trinity)! Cease! Better for you)).[26]

It is worth mentioning that it's important to search for words of the truth by searchers before you and how *they* found the straight path.

((Based on my search for the truth, I concluded that the precise way we believe in God and the deeds we perform determine our future condition for eternity.

If we sincerely seek the truth of this life, which is Islam (peaceful submission to the will of God), God will guide us there, God willing.

He directs us to examine the life and the Sunnah of Prophet Muhammad (peace be upon him), as he represents the best role model for mankind to follow.

Furthermore, God directs us to investigate and ponder what He says in the Qur'an, the last revelation. One will see that the Qur'an is indeed like a persistent and strong knocking on a door. Its loud

---

[26]) Surah 4-171

shouts seek to awaken those who are fast asleep and are completely absorbed by this life on earth.

The knocks and shouts appear one after the other: Wake up! Look around you! Think! Reflect! God is there! There is planning, trial, accountability, reckoning, reward, severe punishment, and everlasting bliss!

Clearly and unequivocally, the best way to live and die in this world is as a righteous Muslim! (Submitted) and (Committed).

When one comes to the conclusion that Islam is the truth, he should not delay in becoming a Muslim because he may die first, and then it will be too late)).[27]

To follow blindly what your grandfathers use to believe is not the way to go. Be yourself as no one can render any help to you in front of Allah on the day of judgment. Search for the truth, create meaning for your life, be sure of your future hereafter, and enjoy the best life before the chance pass away.

---

[27]) See best way to live and die by Yahya Donald Flood

Chapter 5

MANAGING YOUR TIME; EARLY HOURS OF THE DAY - THE MAGIC SECRET OF THE SUCCESS!

It has been stated in the life of Prophet Muhammad (peace be upon him) that he did not like to sleep before Isha (early night prayer), which arises normally around one hour after sunset. Nor did the prophet like to stay awake after this prayer unless some important matter kept him up.

He also used to wake up routinely in the last 1/3 (One third) of the night and pray until the call of the Fajr (morning) prayer, which is approximately one and a half hours before sunrise.

This timing schedule or program was the way of the Prophets (peace be upon them all), and the way of their students and plenty of people in all generations.

The Prophet (peace be upon him) stated that the best way of praying by night and fasting by day, was the way of Prophet Da'ud (David) - peace be upon him -. He used to sleep in the early hours of the night, then wake up from the middle to the late hours of the night. He then rested before he woke up for the early morning prayer before sunrise.

This kind of schedule, no matter how you program it - according to your convenience - makes sure that you sleep enough and wake up early. And we're all aware of how this is ideal for your health, work, achievement, and enjoying life.

The early hours of the day are the best time to achieve good results, execute a good job, and benefit from the time and the environment. One hour of early morning is worth or better than a few hours in the late of the day, and in this way, you keep a happy mood all day and enjoy your life.

Waking up early while most people are sleeping, performing your worship duty, finishing your workout, reading, writing, or working after that, will give you amazing results which you cannot imagine unless you see it practically.

Chapter 6

TRY TO KEEP NATURAL

In everything, always go for the natural choices. Eat naturally, drink naturally. Simply, drinking normal pure natural water is better than drinking colored and flavored ones.

All types of narcotics harm the soul and destroy your health and life. Some might think that it will give happiness and joy, but that couldn't be further from the truth.

Some people think that fun and enjoying life means forgetting the problems and grieves by consuming drugs, alcohol, etc. Again, that is absolutely not true.

These kinds of things are weapons of the devil, the great enemy of the Sons of Adam. How does a person with a functioning mind and powerful thoughts buy into this madness? It's because there is a vacuum inside every human being's soul, and nothing can fill this vacuum except the knowledge and worship of Allah.

Unless the person reaches out for this knowledge, this vacuum will remain and therefore, will be filled by the devil.

((Is he whose breast Allah has opened to Islam, so that he is in light from his Lord "as he who is non-Muslim"?So, woe to those whose hearts are hardened against the remembrance of Allah! They are in plain error)). [28]

The best life is originated at the heart, a piece of flesh. If the heart is good, the whole body will be so. Likewise, if it is ill, then the whole body will be ill.

The person with a heart that fully acknowledges Allah, the Prophet Muhammad - peace be upon him - who lives reciting the Qur'an and acting according to the Qur'an, who remembers Allah day and night and observes his commands, who fulfills his religious duties and avoids prohibited things, will certainly enjoy the best life in any situation, whether he's rich or poor, living the hard life or in luxury, enjoying freedom or locked in a prison.

"If I pay the whole world full of gold to those who prisoned me in this fortress, I cannot reward them for their favor". - Ibnu Tay-miah (died in 799 H).

---

[28]) Surah 39-22

Chapter 7

CONTROL YOUR ANGER

A man asked the Prophet - peace be upon him - to advise him. He said to him in short and one word: "Don't get angry!." Once again, the man again asked for advice. The Prophet said to him: "Don't be angry!" On the third time the Prophet - peace be upon him - said to the man: "Don't get angry and you will enter Jannah (Paradise)".

So why is avoiding anger so important that we were specifically instructed to do so?

It's because anger can drive us to act out of control. An angry person may kill, fight, commit suicide, or do evil things which he might have not considered without feeling angry.

That is why many people when they commit a serious crime, terrible mistakes, or immoral acts, apologize and confess that he or she was angry.

The impact of the acts that come out as a result of anger is not limited to harming other people, but it severely harms the person himself.

The result of the anger is always regret. An angry person can destroy in a minute what has been built for years of hard work.

So, If you want to enjoy your life and feel and taste the best life ever, try your best to be calm and keep away from anger.

In many cases you might be provoked, and come across people with bad behavior, unfair treatment, rude people, and you might feel forced to be angry. However, if you take it easy, deal with coolness, and be careful of your attitude, you will ultimately enjoy life and be the one laughing in the end.

Chapter 8

TELL NO LIES

To say and speak the truth always and in any situation, can make you feel confident and enjoy life. You will not have worries, doubts, or be occupied with hiding contradictions in your life with different people.

Telling the truth doesn't mean volunteering to tell people everything you know, interfering in others' business, or putting your nose up something not related to you.

However, telling the truth of what you have been asked and know for sure, is what we mean. It's being firm and authentic when asked and when the situation is suitable for you to speak out.

Telling the truth automatically leads you to the righteous path. That is why Allah has ordered the believers to say only the truth and to surround themselves with truthful people.

((O you who believe! Be afraid of Allah, and be with those who are true "in words and actions")).29

The Prophet - peace be upon him - stated in one of his traditions:

(Truthfulness leads to Al-Birr (righteousness) and Al-Birr (righteousness) leads to Paradise. And a man keeps on telling the truth until he becomes a truthful person).

All people like the truth but not many speak or practice it. If you give people the truth, eventually it will make them happy. Lies, on the other end, will lead to misery, no matter how good of a liar you think you are. The least price you pay for lying is the time and effort you waste in making your stories add up and covering the lie. That is why Prophet Muhammad peace be upon him said : (Give up what is doubtful to you for that which is not doubtful; for truth is peace of mine and falsehood is doubt". Quoted and authenticated by Imam tirmidi.

Chapter 9

REMEMBER ALLAH, AT ALL TIMES

Those who remember Allah, all the time and in all situations, will verily enjoy life. This type of enjoyment can't be found unless he follows the same path of the piety people.

That is why Allah called his observers to remember him a lot:

((O you who believe! Remember Allah with much remembrance, and glorify His praises morning and afternoon (the early morning and afternoon prayers)).[30]

The Prophet - peace be upon him - has taught the Muslims a supplication of remembering Allah in every aspect and situation. When going to bed, or waking up, or turning up another side in your sleep, before you eat and after you finish, when you wear clothes - especially new ones-, when you go out of the house and when you enter the house, when you ride transportation and when you drive or travel, when you enter the Masjid and when you exit,

---

[30]) Surah 33-(41-42)

when you enter the restroom and when you get out of it, when you enter a new city or a market, in every situation we have a specific supplication to be said.

That means you live with Allah in all your moments and empower yourself with the source of life, the strong power of spirit, which you can use to enforce and strengthen your attitude and character.

This remembrance protects you from the devil and from anything that may harm you like stress, depression, or worries, and gives you peace of mind, happiness, psychological stability and tranquility.

The devil is a dangerous enemy to us, but Allah has given us weapons to fight him and beat him, and he is yet very weak against these weapons unless we don't actually remember to use them.

If we did not use the weapons, the devil will win the battle, and we shall live with grief, and suffer the losses of this battle.

Chapter 10

BE PATIENT

Our whole faith can be divided into two main parts. The first half is Patience, and the other half is thanking. In reality, our whole lif is divided in to these two parts: things that make you happy, which you give thanks for, and other things that cause you grief, for which you must have Patience.

Patience is power. No success can be achieved without it. The difference between achievements and failures, winners and losers, is patience.

In the Qur'an, we find more than One hundred verses ordering or instructing or advising us to be patient enough to see the good results.

Prophet Muhammad - peace be upon him - stayed in Makkah for 13 years under the oppression and atrocities of his own tribe.

He tried to seek refuge and protection from the people of Taif after the death of his wife Khadija and his uncle Abu-Talib, but they rejected him and threw stones on him until his feet were bleeding.

All the prophets - peace be upon them - Abraham, Moses, Jesus, Joseph, and others were in a high level of patience in order to convey the message and to feel and taste good life under the pressure of the transgressors, polytheists, and nonbelievers of their time.

But ultimately they succeed and achieved their goals, completed their message, and enjoyed their life under the direct connection to Allah Almighty. Eventually, they paved the way for the seekers and searchers of the best life.

You need patience in every step of your life. In education, work, social life, the street, and in dealing with different people and everyday processes of life.

Life is a long journey and needs the patience to cut the distance of years. You will never find everything to your like, whether that's in the people around you or in different situations of your life.

Patience is your key to staying firm and focused, to continue your journey with health and happiness, learning from losses, mistakes, and failures, and turning them into success stories and experiences. All this is done while keeping in mind that it is not the end, and life will not stop for your sake.

Whether you choose to kill yourself or live battling your grief and sorrow whether you continue the struggle or step up aside from the race, whether you do or die, life stops for nobody. It will move and continue moving, whether you stay onboard or stay out of it.

Therefore, be patient, practice this patience in whatever situation you're facing. Always choose to keep going and to enjoy this life until the end of your days.

Eventually, you will disappear, but your impact and influence will remain. It may stay behind you for years and centuries, and it can motivate millions and millions, in different generations and places, so they too, can move in life with patience and enjoy their short time on this planet.

Chapter 11

HAVE A GIVING SPIRIT

Being charitable for those in need, for good causes, for making the life of others better, will make your *own* life feel more wonderful and more meaningful.

It is not a matter of having more or fewer amounts. It is a matter of giving until it becomes an intrinsic habit.

In the Qur'an we have hundreds of verses encouraging people to give charity and help the needy.

(Those who spend their wealth for the cause of Allah and afterward make not reproach and injury to follow that which they have spent; their reward is with their lord, and there shall no fear come upon them, neither shall they grieve)) Sura: 2 verse: 262

Researches proof that giving charity makes you live longer, happier, and healthier.

"Generosity may be a 'magic pill' for happiness and longevity" The Seattle Times published an article in this title on August 30, 2015.[31]

"Many studies have found that generosity, both volunteering, and charitable donations, benefits young and old physically and psychologically".

"The benefits of giving are significant, according to those studies: lower blood pressure, lower risk of dementia, less anxiety and depression, reduced cardiovascular risk and overall greater happiness"[32]

"Many studies show that one of the best ways to deal with the hardships in life is not to just center on yourself but to take the opportunity to engage in simple acts of kindness"

"Studies show that when people think about helping others, they activate a part of the brain called the mesolimbic pathway, which is responsible for feelings of gratification. Helping others doles out happiness chemicals, including dopamine, endorphins that block pain signals and oxytocin, known as the tranquility hormone".[33]

---

[31]) https://www.seattletimes.com/life/wellness/generosity-may-be-a-magic-pill-for-happiness-and-longevity/
[32]) same source
[33]) same above source

Whenever you give, and whatever good you do, you will get rewarded. You may see this reward soon, and you may have to wait to see it later.

It is the fairness of Allah, that He accounts for you every good action you do in this world. He never ignores or overlooks any single good act you do.

Chapter 12

BE FAIR... TREAT OTHERS AS YOU LIKE TO BE TREATED

Without a doubt, every one of us would like to be honored, respected, and treated in a good manner. The good news is, you can probably get this result by simply treating others in honor, respect, and good behavior.

Always imagine yourself on the other side, and you will find yourself automatically closer to fairness in treating and dealing with others.

Prophet Muhammad, peace be upon him, teaching us good manners and behaviors, said in a clear Hadith: (… and person should treat the people as he like them to treat him).

Chapter 13

THE WORLD IS LARGE... THINK BIG

(My believing servants! My earth is indeed vast. You should worship me and me alone). Sura 29, verse 56.

The World, in which we live, is large enough. If an opportunity is missed in one place, you can try moving to another one. The secret is that you know Allah, who created you, and created this vast earth, and you live with him by remembering him all time.

Your land is where your opportunity lies. Where you can achieve your ambitions and dreams. It is not only where you are named or labeled.

This is how things work. If you take a look at the world today, you will find many people who achieved their dreams in a different place than their place of origin.

At the end, you only live only one life, try to make it better in grasping your opportunities as they pass you in place. Usually, opportunities come once a while, and if you did not benefit from it at the time, it will immediately disappear and will not wait for you for a long time.

Chapter 14

OPPORTUNITIES NEVER END

Some people feel grieved, stressed, and depressed if they cannot meet success on their first or second, or even third try. They may hate their own life, envy others who got the wealth or job or happiness that they seek. However, that is absolutely not the solution or the way of healthy thinking.

You must know that opportunities have no limits and no end. However, it also requires some effort, optimism, patience, and a smart way of thinking or working from your end.

The World is full of opportunities, and it is distributed to almost every corner of the world.

Some of the wealthiest countries in the world have no natural resources but still achieved incredible success in their economical and industrial development. While some countries are full of natural resources but are still living in some of the worst economic and social situations because of manmade disasters of corruption, lack of governance, bad leadership, and management. Still, it is a matter of how to utilize your opportunities.

You should never give up on yourself, working hard and continuing to try. If you stop trying and lose hope, there's a zero precent chance of success, but if you keep going despite all odds, you have a shot at succeeding and winning one day.

The Qur'an tells us the story of Jacob and Joseph in a marvelous way, and although Jacob lost his two sons Joseph and Benjamin one after other, he never lost hope and said in his supplication:

((.. Patience is most befitting (for me); maybe Allah will bring them back to me altogether; surely He is the All-knowing, the Truly Wise)). Sura Yusuf 12, verse 83.

And that is what eventually happened when he met with his two sons after many years.

He even encouraged his other sons to look around and enquire about their lost brothers:

((O my sons! Go and inquire about Joseph and his brother (Benjamin), and despair not of Allah's Mercy; surely non despair Allah's Mercy except the disbelieving people)). Sura yusuf 12, verse 87.

Chapter 15

PLAN YOUR GOALS

You must plan your Goals in life, in order to live a meaningful life and spend your time in something you like to do and actually want to work for.

When you have goals to achieve, a list of things to do every day, every new day in your life is seen as an opportunity to develop your goals and succeed in your efforts. Likewise, when you have no written or listed goals to achieve in this world you may end up somewhere unfamiliar to your dreams or likes.

Living for a message and for a goal, naturally transforms you into an energetic workaholic, who is inspired and committed to doing his job perfectly in the best way he can.

Chapter 16

LEARN FROM HISTORY

Always be a good reader of history and grasp the lessons of what happened to those who came before you and before your time.

You are One among a big family called the human beings, children of Adam, who live together on this planet, regardless of their color, faith, language, ethnicity, or location.

All of them are of the same origin, and all their files are in one place and managed from one admin. The life and stories of all of them are stored in history. If You are a king, scientist, businessman, traveler, writer, poet, singer, doctor, or in any field, there are so many like you who came before you. From your end, you just need to open a part of these records and check the experience and similarities, the identical pictures and life, of those who looked like you or were in your same situation and position and find out where they ended.

Chapter 17

INCREASE YOUR KNOWLEDGE EVERY DAY

L earning never ends and has no limit. If you stop learning, you stop leading a good life. Learn, read, travel, talk to people, look around, think positively, use your talents and harness your memory of storing information and knowledge, utilize it in the best way you can.

The small memory slot in your body can store millions and trillions of pictures, stories, numbers, and information. It is all dependent on how you utilize it, how far you use it, how you benefit from it.

You can use 100 GB, and you can use 1000 TB. Whenever you read or see or listen to something new, it will add to its field and department of information and knowledge. When you want to recall it, anywhere and at any time, it will take seconds to rush to you with the stored information as fresh as if you had planted it today.

This is a blessing from Allah, that he gave the human being what he did not give to all other creations. That is the ability of endless knowledge, information, and expression of names and pictures as it is. He taught it to Adam, the father of all humans, and he gifted it to every newborn of his children.

For example, take a look at the language. All people speak countless languages in different places in this world, but they learned certain languages that dominated the knowledge of their whole world. It is how they exported and spread their language.

The English Language was born on a small island in Europe, but It became in so many centuries the mother language of knowledge and understanding each other all over the world.

The English-speaking people were smart enough, in my opinion, to export the best product they had, their own language throughout the whole world. It was not only the colonial influence that made the English language the number one international language. Other languages like French and Portuguese led colonized nations to spread their language to many parts of the world but did not have the same impact that the English language did.

Therefore, some other factors were crucial for the language to dominate.

But the question is how you can seek and increase your knowledge every day?

Chapter 18

KEEP GOING & NEVER QUIT!

Every day you may encounter some troubles, turbulences, confusion, and situations that make you nervous or upset.

Take it easy and never feel overwhelmed. It is not worth it to mess up your life for something you cannot avoid or control. You must try to change it to the best in the easiest way, and if you did not succeed, for now, it is not the end, you can try another time. In the end, keeping on your trials is the meaning of life.

You have simply to realize that whatever situation you're in is not the end. Whether you are denied by your right, or you missed the plane or the bus for an important appointment! It's not the end of your application for a job that was rejected! It's not the end if you lost the one you love or if you were betrayed by someone close!

You were disappointed with a friend? So what! It is terrible, but it cannot stop you from moving forward. Take the Lessons and experiences, and decide to keep going.

" Probably the greatest example of persistence is Abraham Lincoln. If you want to learn about somebody who didn't quit, look no further.

Born into poverty, Lincoln was faced with defeat throughout his life. He lost eight elections, failed twice in business, and suffered a nervous breakdown.

He could have quit many times - but he didn't and because he didn't quit, he became one of the greatest presidents in the history of the United States.

Lincoln was a champion, and he never gave up. Here is a sketch of Lincoln's Road to the white house:

- 1816: His family was forced out of their home. He had to work to support them.
- 1818: His mother died.
- 1831: Failed in business.
- 1832: Run for state legislature - lost.
- 1832: Also lost his job - wanted to go to law school but couldn't get in.
- 1833: Borrowed some money from a friend to begin a business and by the end of the year he was bankrupt. He spent the next 17 years of his life paying off this debt.
- 1834: Run for state legislature again - won.

- 1835: Was engaged to be married, but his sweetheart died and his heart was broken.

- 1836: Had a total nervous breakdown and was in bed for six months.

- 1838: Sought to become speaker of the state legislature- was defeated.

- 1840: Sought to become elector - was defeated.

- 1843: Run for Congress - lost.

- 1846: Run for Congress again - this time he won - went to Washington and did a good job.

- 1848: Run for re-election to Congress - lost.

- 1849: Sought the job of land officer in his home state - rejected.

- 1854: Run for Senate of the United States - lost.

- 1856: Sought the Vice-Presidential nomination at his party's national convention - got less than 100 votes.

- 1858: Run for U.S. Senate again - lost.

- 1860: Elected President of the United States.[34]

That is a small reward for someone who never quits.

---

[34] snopes.com web site, article David Mikkelson, 12/7/2000

Chapter 19

CHOOSE YOUR WORDS!

A lways speak in a good manner. Choose and pick your words like choosing a good-looking piece of fruit. Whatever the situation might be, train yourself to be calm and collected, managing your feelings throughout the whole thing.

The more you speak well the more you can feel happy and enjoy life. The words that come from you might not have a strong impact or offense on the other party, but they will definitely have a strong impact on you first.

(*And tell My servants to say that which is best. Indeed, Satan induces [dissension] among them. Indeed Satan is ever, to mankind, a clear enemy.*). [Al-Isr'ā: 53]

It is a very simple formula. When you speak well you are the first one to get the benefit. You feel peaceful, you feel happy and satisfied, and you might even feel proud of your control and discipline.

(..... *And Speak to People good (words)...*) Al-Isra: 83

To all people regardless of color, religion, language, or any other particularity. That is the way to peaceful life and true happiness.

Chapter 20

PROTECT YOUR SOUL FROM ENVY & STINGINESS

(... And whoever is protected from the stinginess of his soul - it is those who will be successful.). Al-hashr - 9

It is a matter of heart not body. Clean hearts, empty of any kind of envy or hatred are the ones that can enjoy a better life and stay happy.

They don't concern themselves with what others are being granted or given. They think about their own blessing and mind their own business. This small, small flesh in our chest is the most important organ in our body.

It is the store of every feeling, every decision, every gesture, and every move we make. It is the laboratory and the factory that analyzes and evaluate everything we see or hear.

If you make it a point to keep your heart clean and healthy, you will feel the taste of happiness in your whole life.

The Final Note

FOR YOUR HEART

The conclusion of this topic is that the best life which everybody is looking for cannot be found unless the person submits himself totally and sincerely to his Creator, provider, the Only Sustainer, Allah. He is the Creator of the Heavens, the Earth, and the Man.

There is no other way you can feel and enjoy life, without truly believing in Allah, his Messenger Muhammad and all previous Messengers peace be upon them all, his Books - All his books - his Angels, The day of resurrection in the hereafter, and the Divine good or bad.

You must have knowledge in Allah, his names, his attributes, his greatness, his eternal power, and his creation of decision of everything.

You have to search for the truth and believe in the Final Messenger of Allah, the Seal of the Prophets, Muhammad - peace be upon him - and in his religion that concluded the previous religions.

You have to have faith in the book which he brought to us, the Qur'an, that covered and compiled the content of all previous books, including the Tawrah and the Gospel, in order to enable you to enjoy your life.

Every human being must believe in this faith in order to save himself from the Hellfire. No one can buy this faith; No one can give it to another, it is a blessed selection and gift from Allah. There are some great Prophets - peace be upon them - who could not grant it to their children or wife.

If you read the Qur'an and the history, you will know that the Prophets of Allah, like Noah, Ibrahim, Muhammad - peace be upon them - could not give the faith, the belief in Allah and the gift of worshipping him alone, to their close relatives, no matter how much they wanted to.

Noah could not give to his son or his wife, and they eventually died as unbelievers. Ibrahim could not give to his own father. Muhammad - peace be upon them - could not give to his uncles.

To believe in Allah, to have knowledge in Him, to know his true religion, to get the straight path to Paradise, to get and enjoy the best life, is a privilege, and you must search sincerely for this true belief in Islamic Monotheism.

Just open your mind, clean your heart, give a chance to your judgment, and think big, out of your box, put the assumptions and pre-perceptions aside, and then decide. No pressure and no compulsion.

This is your own responsibility. Your own future and your own eternal life hereafter. Nobody else, no matter who they are, can decide it for you. You must decide it for yourself, because no one walks with you to the end of your life, beyond the grave, no matter how much he loves you.

Your children, your wife, your friends, your husband, your relatives and colleagues, all of them will look after their own selves, and leave you alone to your last destination in this life.

But from there you will start another phase of life, and another journey, either to Paradise or to Hell. Today is the Chance to make a decision and do good deeds, tomorrow in the hereafter is for being held accountable for your choice.

You have a choice to make, whether you will try to be sincere and truthful to yourself, or to cheat yourself and rely on your old fathers and their says as the Qur'an already taught us:

((We found our fathers following a certain way and religion, and we will indeed follow their footsteps)).[35]

Whether you already believe in Allah and in His Messenger Muhammad - peace be upon him - and simply need to renew your

---

[35]) Surah 43-23

faith and follow it with good deeds, or perhaps you don't believe in Allah and his Messenger Muhammad - peace be upon him - and need to study, review, think and decide; you have to eventually follow the Quran and the Sunnah - the way of Prophet Muhammad - peace be upon him - in order to enjoy your life in here and in the hereafter.

The Qur'an clearly and explicitly explains:

((There is no compulsion in religion. Verily, the Right Path has become distinct from the Wrong Path. Whoever disbelieves in Taghut "anything worshipped other than the Real God - Allah" and believes in Allah, then he has grasped the most trustworthy handhold that will never break. And Allah is All-Hearer, All Knower)). [36]

---

[36]) Surah 2-256

Printed in Great Britain
by Amazon